I0846224

The Little Town

LOGAN PAUL WYSE

The story
of a Scientist,
a Farmer,
and a Town.

For Lydia and Erica
*Thanks for not letting me be
a 'stuffy Architect"*

based on a
hopefully soon to be
true story.

Resting on the coast of a tranquil
lake lies the C between A and B.

A bustling Town of interaction and
conversation.

Each individual a participant,
each interaction adding to the total
identity of the Town.

But this was not always so...

In its past the little Town was isolated. A
pit stop of sorts for travelers and tourists
on their way to destination B.

The inhabitants of this little Town payed
no mind to the visitors from destination A.

They went about their daily lives rarely
encountering another soul they had not met
before.

The tragedy lies in invisible,
the could have been, the what if, the if only.

The story goes that a
scientist from the Big City
stopped for fuel at the
little Town.

He was on his way to give
an important lecture at
the College of B.

He stands there flustered
as he is baffled at his latest
earth saving problem of
trying to create a better
way of growing crops.

In his frustration he quickly refuels and heads
out of Town speeding past a local diner.

Unknown to the scientist however was
the existence of a local farmer enjoying
his lunch at the diner.

He, who has been trying
to tackle the exact same
earth saving problem, drank
his afternoon coffee, quite
annoyed at the speed of
a particular vehicle that
roared passed the diner a
few moments ago…

What neither of them could perceive was that the information held in the mind of the scientist from the big city was exactly what was missing from the mind of the farmer from our little Town.

And the information that
was held in the mind of
the Farmer was exactly
what was missing from
the mind of the scientist.

But alas, the scientist gave
is lecture, and the farmer
continued farming,
neither one of them aware
of the others presence.

But the Town noticed this interaction,
or lack thereof, along with thousands
of other missed interactions between
travelers, locals, and visitors.

The Town was furious at how simply
the shape and organization of its streets
and structures so many experience and
interactions could be missed.

Then an idea occurred to the Town...

"If they wont talk, and they wont share, then I
will change so they meet here."

At once, though very slowly, the Town
began to change. Where a small area
of beach was, barely enough for two
people, an enormous sand dune arose.
Rising from out of the little lake, the
dune threatened to swallow the Town.

Then, the ground beneath the scattered main
street began to shift and change. The Town, being
very slow and deliberate as not to damage or
destroy any of the buildings, began to bring all the
structures together to the heart of the town.

The roads that used to be straight and fast
began to shift and bow causing traffic,
including the speedy scientist, to slow as they
approached.

Restaurants, boutiques, grocers, shops, homes and
everything else were shifted and stacked to create a
interwoven network of neighbors and businesses.

The imposing dune now threatened
to swallowed the now semi circular
town. So the inhabitants, much to the
Towns delight, dug connecting tunnels
through the dune to the coast of the
tranquil lake. These tunnels connected
businesses to businesses, plazas to
plazas, water ways to water ways.

Now, with the Towns work done, it
looked to see a speedy car approaching
from the Big City. This was the scientist
who was stopping to recharge his vehicle
at the not so little Town on his way to
give an important lecture at the College
of C. Upon his speedy approach he
slowed to a crawl to observe the dynamic
and rare sight of the town.

His road split without warning and he
was led down into the dune where he
was parked at a local diner at the same
table as a particularly dirty fellow who
was enjoying a cup of coffee.

The scientist rolled down his window and when the server approached, he asked the gentleman politely to order him a coffee.

As the sun set on the not so little Town, the lamps were lit, and the plazas filled with locals, visitors, and travelers alike. Everyone enjoying not only the sights, smells, and attractions of the Town, but more importantly the interactions that made them all possible.

The End.

9 781716 652608